LEAD LIKE A PRO: MASTER THE SKILLS OF EFFECTIVE LEADERSHIP

1. Introduction: The Art and Science of Leadership
2. Chapter 1: Understanding Your Leadership Style
3. Chapter 2: Emotional Intelligence (EQ) – The Foundation of Great Leadership
4. Chapter 3: Building Trust and Credibility
5. Chapter 4: Mastering Communication Skills for Leaders
6. Chapter 5: Decision Making and Problem Solving as a Leader
7. Chapter 6: Leading Through Change and Uncertainty
8. Chapter 7: Motivating and Inspiring Your Team
9. Chapter 8: Delegation and Empowerment
10. Chapter 9: Conflict Resolution and Difficult Conversations
11. Chapter 10: Continuous Learning and Self-Improvement
12. Conclusion: Becoming a Pro-Level Leader

INTRODUCTION: THE ART AND SCIENCE OF LEADERSHIP

In today's fast-paced world, leadership has never been more important—or more challenging. As businesses evolve, teams grow more diverse, and technologies advance, the need for effective leadership stands at the forefront of success. However, the concept of leadership is often misunderstood. People tend to confuse it with mere management, thinking it's about telling others what to do, keeping things in order, or making sure tasks are completed on time. But true leadership is much more than that. Leadership is both an art and a science—a delicate balance between human connection and strategic thinking. It's about inspiring people to achieve more than they ever thought possible and guiding them through difficult times with confidence and clarity.

In this introduction, we'll explore what leadership truly means in our modern world, why it's more complex than simply being in charge, and how understanding both the "art" and the "science" behind it can help you become an exceptional leader.

THE DIFFERENCE BETWEEN LEADERSHIP AND MANAGEMENT

The terms "leadership" and "management" are often used interchangeably, but they are not the same thing. Management is about maintaining control—organising tasks, allocating resources, and ensuring that day-to-day operations run smoothly. While management is essential for any functioning organisation, leadership is what takes things to the next level. Leadership is not just about managing tasks or telling people what to do. Instead, it's about vision and influence. Leaders inspire people, set direction, and motivate teams to reach higher goals.

Consider this: a manager might ensure that a project stays on track by setting deadlines, assigning tasks, and following up on progress. A leader, on the other hand, will make sure that the team understands why the project matters. They'll inspire the team to invest their energy and creativity into the project, even in the face of challenges. The leader creates a sense of purpose, aligning each member's personal motivations with the overall goal. While management ensures efficiency, leadership fosters growth, innovation, and a shared commitment to success.

In simple terms, management is about "doing things right," while leadership is about "doing the right things." Both are necessary, but leadership is what inspires change and transformation.

WHY LEADERSHIP IS CRUCIAL IN TODAY'S WORLD

The world is changing at an unprecedented pace. New technologies disrupt industries every day, and the workforce is more diverse, globalised, and interconnected than ever before. Teams aren't just confined to an office—they span continents, working remotely, sometimes without ever meeting face-to-face. As these dynamics shift, traditional management approaches are becoming less effective. People crave something more from their leaders. They want to feel heard, valued, and connected. They want a sense of purpose in their work, and they want leaders who can guide them through uncertain times.

In times of crisis, strong leadership becomes even more critical. Whether it's navigating through a global pandemic, handling economic downturns, or facing unexpected competition, the ability to lead effectively can make the difference between failure and success. Leadership is what helps teams stay focused when everything else is in chaos. It builds resilience and provides a clear path forward when the road is unclear.

More than ever, leadership is about adaptability. It's about being able to change course when necessary, respond to new challenges, and inspire others to do the same. Leaders must be able to engage with the emotional and practical needs of their teams, striking the perfect balance between empathy and decisiveness.

THE ART OF LEADERSHIP: LEADING WITH HEART

Now, let's delve into the "art" of leadership. Leadership, at its core, is about people. It's about understanding the human side of those you lead—their emotions, motivations, strengths, and challenges. A great leader knows how to connect on a personal level, making people feel seen and valued. This is where emotional intelligence comes into play. Leaders who are emotionally intelligent are able to navigate the complexities of human emotions, fostering trust and building strong relationships with their teams.

Being a leader requires intuition, empathy, and creativity. It's the ability to sense when someone needs encouragement or when to push them harder. It's knowing how to communicate in a way that resonates with individuals, while still maintaining the cohesion of the whole group. These qualities can't always be measured or put into a formula. This is what makes leadership an art. Great leaders inspire not because they follow a rigid set of rules, but because they know how to tap into the human spirit.

Think of iconic leaders like Martin Luther King Jr. or Mahatma Gandhi. They weren't just managing movements—they were leading people with vision, compassion, and heart. They understood that leadership is about more than just achieving goals. It's about inspiring change, creating hope, and leaving a lasting legacy.

In your journey to becoming a great leader, mastering this art—this human connection—is crucial. You must learn to lead with heart, to care deeply about the people you guide, and to foster a sense of belonging and trust. This will make you not only a more effective leader but also a leader people want to follow.

THE SCIENCE OF LEADERSHIP: STRATEGY, STRUCTURE, AND SYSTEMS

While the "art" of leadership focuses on human connection, the "science" of leadership is rooted in logic, systems, and strategy. Leadership is not just about gut feelings or emotional intuition; it also requires concrete skills, strategic planning, and evidence-based decision-making. This is the part of leadership where data, analytics, and frameworks come into play.

Great leaders don't rely solely on instinct—they use proven methods and techniques to make informed decisions. They understand how to set clear objectives, measure progress, and create efficient systems that help their teams achieve success. A leader who only focuses on inspiration without the necessary structures in place will struggle to sustain long-term success. The science of leadership provides the foundation upon which the art can thrive.

The scientific side of leadership includes areas such as:

Strategic Planning: Knowing how to set long-term goals, create actionable plans, and adapt strategies as circumstances change.

Problem-Solving: Analysing situations objectively, considering multiple perspectives, and making decisions based on logic and data.

Delegation: Effectively assigning tasks to the right people, ensuring that the team's strengths are maximised and resources are used efficiently.

Time Management: Prioritising tasks, setting deadlines, and ensuring that the team remains focused on high-impact activities.

Just as artists learn techniques and musicians practice scales, leaders must also develop a set of practical, scientific skills that can be applied consistently. This balance of art and science is what sets great leaders apart from good ones. To be successful, you need both. You need to inspire people and motivate them to action, but you also need to have the systems in place to guide them towards success.

THE LEADERSHIP JOURNEY: A LIFELONG LEARNING PROCESS

Becoming a great leader is not a one-time achievement—it's a lifelong journey. Leadership is not something you either have or don't have. It's a skill, a mindset, and a way of being that you can develop and refine over time. Every experience you encounter, every success and failure, contributes to your growth as a leader.

The best leaders never stop learning. They seek out feedback, challenge themselves to grow, and continually refine their skills. They are humble enough to recognize their limitations and curious enough to keep improving. Whether you're leading a small team or running a large organisation, the journey to leadership excellence is never over. The more you invest in your leadership abilities, the more your team and organisation will thrive.

In the pages that follow, we'll dive deep into both the art and science of leadership, equipping you with the tools, techniques, and insights needed to lead with confidence and effectiveness. You'll learn how to understand your leadership style, communicate with impact, make smart decisions, and inspire those around you to reach their highest potential. You'll also be challenged to reflect on your own growth, applying the concepts to real-world situations in your life and work.

As you embark on this journey, remember: leadership is not about being perfect. It's about being authentic, adaptable, and willing to grow. Through dedication and practice, you can lead like a pro.

CHAPTER 1: UNDERSTANDING YOUR LEADERSHIP STYLE

Leadership is not a one-size-fits-all role. Every person has their unique way of leading, shaped by their personality, experiences, values, and the people around them. Some leaders are naturally more direct and decisive, while others prefer to lead by listening and building consensus. The key to becoming an effective leader is to understand your own leadership style and leverage it in a way that brings out the best in both you and your team.

This chapter is dedicated to helping you identify, explore, and refine your leadership style. By understanding how you naturally lead, you can become more self-aware, more adaptable, and ultimately more successful in guiding others. We'll also discuss the importance of flexibility and growth, as even the best leaders must adapt their style based on the needs of their team and the challenges they face.

WHAT IS A LEADERSHIP STYLE?

At its core, your leadership style is the way you approach leading others. It's a combination of your behaviour, communication style, decision-making process, and the way you motivate and interact with your team. Just like personal style, leadership style is shaped by who you are—your personality, strengths, and even your weaknesses. The way you handle problems, communicate under pressure, and inspire your team all contribute to your overall leadership approach.

While every leader is unique, leadership styles can generally be categorised into different types. These categories serve as a useful framework for understanding how you tend to lead and where you might want to make adjustments. However, remember that these styles aren't rigid boxes. You may find that you use different aspects of multiple styles depending on the situation.

COMMON LEADERSHIP STYLES

Here's an overview of some common leadership styles. As you read through them, think about which one resonates with you the most. Which behaviours and traits do you notice in your own leadership?

Autocratic Leadership
Autocratic leaders make decisions independently, often without consulting others. They are highly directive and expect their team to follow instructions without much debate or input. This style can be effective in situations that require quick decision-making, like during a crisis, but it may stifle creativity and leave team members feeling disempowered.

Example: Think of a military general who gives orders, and the team is expected to follow them immediately. There's little room for discussion in these moments because efficiency and precision are crucial.

Democratic Leadership
Democratic leaders value input from their team and make decisions collaboratively. They believe in fostering an environment where everyone's opinions are heard, and decisions are made based on group consensus. This style often leads to more creative solutions and a greater sense of ownership among team members. However, it can slow down the decision-making process, especially in time-sensitive situations.

Example: A startup founder who gathers the entire team to brainstorm new product features, encouraging everyone to share their thoughts before making the final decision.

Transformational Leadership

Transformational leaders are visionaries who inspire and motivate their team to strive for greatness. They focus on long-term goals, personal growth, and positive change, often pushing their team to exceed their own expectations. These leaders are charismatic and passionate, creating a sense of purpose in their followers. However, this style can sometimes overlook the day-to-day needs of the team, as the focus is often on the bigger picture.

Example: A CEO who continually motivates their company with a vision of revolutionising the industry, pushing employees to innovate and think outside the box.

Laissez-Faire Leadership

Laissez-faire leaders take a hands-off approach, giving their team a lot of freedom to make decisions and work independently. This style can be empowering for teams that are highly skilled and self-motivated, but it can lead to chaos or lack of direction if the team lacks experience or guidance

Example: A project manager who allows their team to set their own deadlines and manage their own tasks, only stepping in when necessary.

Servant Leadership

Servant leaders prioritise the needs of their team above their own. They focus on serving others, ensuring their team has the resources, support, and guidance they need to succeed. This style fosters a strong sense of trust and loyalty, but it can sometimes lead to the leader neglecting their own well-being or overextending themselves.

Example: A leader who goes out of their way to help their team members with personal development, making sure they have everything they need to succeed, even if it means putting their own needs on hold.

Transactional Leadership

Transactional leaders operate on a system of rewards and consequences. They set clear expectations and provide incentives for meeting those expectations. This style is often focused on performance and efficiency. While it can be effective in certain environments, it may not inspire innovation or long-term growth.

Example: A sales manager who sets monthly sales targets and offers bonuses for those who meet them, while also enforcing penalties for underperformance.

DISCOVERING YOUR LEADERSHIP STYLE

So, how do you figure out what your leadership style is? The best way is through self-reflection, feedback from others, and observation. Here are some steps to help you discover and refine your leadership style:

Self-Reflection
Start by thinking about your natural tendencies when leading others. Do you prefer to make decisions on your own, or do you seek input from others? Are you more focused on the big picture, or do you tend to get involved in the details? Reflect on how you handle conflict, how you communicate, and what motivates you as a leader.

Gather Feedback
Sometimes, it's hard to see ourselves objectively. That's why it's important to seek feedback from the people you lead. Ask your team for honest input about your leadership style. Do they feel empowered? Supported? Micromanaged? Getting feedback can give you valuable insight into how your leadership is perceived by others.

Analyse Your Past Leadership Experiences
Think about specific situations where you've taken on a leadership role. What approach did you take? What worked well, and what didn't? Were there moments where you felt particularly effective or moments where you struggled? Analysing past experiences can help you identify patterns in your leadership style.

Consider Your Strengths and Weaknesses

Every leader has strengths and areas for improvement. Understanding these can help you refine your leadership style. For example, if you're naturally decisive, you might be strong in crisis situations but need to work on being more inclusive in decision-making. If you're highly empathetic, you might excel at building relationships but struggle with setting firm boundaries.

ADAPTING AND EVOLVING YOUR LEADERSHIP STYLE

While it's important to understand your natural leadership style, great leaders know that adaptability is key. Different situations and teams require different approaches. A team of experienced professionals may thrive under a laissez-faire leader, while a group of newer employees might need more direction and structure.

Consider leadership as a toolkit—you have a set of tools (styles) at your disposal, and your job is to use the right one for the situation. There will be times when you need to be more direct, times when collaboration is essential, and moments when inspiring a vision is what will move the team forward.

Here are a few tips for adapting your leadership style:

Know Your Team: Understand the needs, strengths, and challenges of the people you're leading. Adjust your style to meet them where they are.

Assess the Situation: In high-stress situations, you might need to be more decisive. In creative environments, a more democratic approach may work best.

Be Open to Feedback: Leadership is a constant learning process. Be open to feedback and willing to make adjustments as needed.

Commit to Growth: Great leaders are always evolving. Stay committed to your personal and professional growth as a leader.

HOMEWORK: DISCOVERING YOUR LEADERSHIP STYLE

Reflect: Take 10-15 minutes to reflect on a recent situation where you took a leadership role. Write down your thoughts on the following questions:

How did you approach the situation?

What leadership style did you naturally use?

What went well, and what could have been done differently?

Ask for Feedback: Reach out to two people who have experienced your leadership (coworkers, team members, etc.). Ask them to share their thoughts on your leadership style and provide one piece of constructive feedback.

Take a Leadership Style Quiz: There are many free quizzes online that can help you identify your leadership style. Find one that resonates with you and take the quiz. Compare the results to your own reflections—do they match up?

Set a Goal: Based on your reflections and feedback, set one goal for improving your leadership style. This could be something like "Involve my team more in decision-making" or "Work on being more decisive in high-pressure situations." Write this goal down and revisit it regularly.

CHAPTER 2: EMOTIONAL INTELLIGENCE (EQ) – THE FOUNDATION OF GREAT LEADERSHIP

When people think of leadership, they often picture qualities like decisiveness, vision, or authority. While these traits are important, one of the most crucial components of great leadership is something that is often overlooked: Emotional Intelligence (EQ).

EQ is the ability to understand, manage, and influence not only your own emotions but also the emotions of others. It's about being self-aware, empathetic, and socially aware, which helps leaders to build stronger relationships, navigate conflicts effectively, and inspire their teams. Leaders with high emotional intelligence can create a positive work environment, foster loyalty, and encourage a sense of belonging in their teams.

In this chapter, we'll dive deep into what emotional intelligence is, why it's vital for leadership, and how you can develop your EQ to become a more effective and empathetic leader.

WHAT IS EMOTIONAL INTELLIGENCE?

Emotional intelligence refers to the ability to recognize and regulate your own emotions and the emotions of others. Unlike IQ, which measures cognitive ability, EQ measures your emotional awareness and capacity to handle interpersonal dynamics. In leadership, EQ is essential because leading people is not just about giving directions or making decisions—it's about understanding and motivating them, resolving conflicts, and building trust.

There are five core components of emotional intelligence that are especially important for leaders:

Self-Awareness
Self-awareness is the ability to recognize and understand your emotions and how they affect your thoughts and behaviour. Leaders who are self-aware are conscious of their emotional responses and how these can impact their decision-making, communication, and interactions with their team.
Example: Imagine a leader who feels frustrated after a meeting didn't go well. A self-aware leader would acknowledge that frustration and take a step back before reacting, ensuring their emotions don't cloud their judgement.

Self-Regulation
Self-regulation refers to your ability to control or redirect disruptive emotions and impulses. Leaders who are able to self-regulate can stay calm under pressure and avoid making impulsive decisions. This creates an environment of trust and

dependability because their team knows they won't overreact or lose control in difficult situations.

Example: A leader facing a tight deadline might feel overwhelmed. Instead of snapping at their team, they would pause, collect their thoughts, and approach the situation with a clear head.

Motivation

Emotionally intelligent leaders are highly motivated, not just by external rewards like money or status, but by a deeper desire to achieve personal growth, long-term goals, and make a positive impact. Their passion for their work is contagious, inspiring their team to stay committed and motivated even when things get tough.

Example: A leader working on a challenging project might express their genuine excitement for the project's potential impact, encouraging the team to push through difficulties.

Empathy

Empathy is the ability to understand and share the feelings of others. Leaders who are empathetic can sense what their team members are feeling and respond in a way that shows understanding and compassion. Empathy helps to build strong relationships, reduce conflicts, and foster a sense of belonging.

Example: When a team member seems disengaged or stressed, an empathetic leader would take the time to talk to them, listen to their concerns, and offer support rather than assuming they're simply not performing.

Social Skills

Social skills involve your ability to manage relationships, communicate effectively, and build networks. Leaders with strong social skills can inspire and influence others, resolve conflicts, and create a collaborative environment. This is crucial for creating a positive team culture and ensuring smooth operations.

Example: A leader who is adept at communication might hold regular one-on-one meetings to ensure each team member feels heard and valued, fostering a more open and productive work environment.

WHY EQ MATTERS IN LEADERSHIP

Now that we've outlined the components of emotional intelligence, let's discuss why EQ is so crucial for leadership. While technical skills and expertise are important, the ability to manage emotions and relationships can often determine whether a leader succeeds or fails. Here's why:

Building Stronger Relationships
Leadership is about working with people, and relationships are at the heart of effective leadership. Leaders with high EQ can build trust, create open communication, and develop strong relationships with their team members. This helps to create a work environment where people feel valued, heard, and motivated to contribute their best.

Conflict Resolution
In any workplace, conflict is inevitable. Emotionally intelligent leaders are better equipped to handle conflicts because they can navigate emotionally charged situations with empathy and self-regulation. They're able to diffuse tension, listen to different perspectives, and find solutions that respect everyone's feelings and needs.

Creating a Positive Work Environment
Leaders set the tone for their team. Those with high EQ can foster an environment of positivity and collaboration, where team members feel comfortable taking risks, sharing ideas, and growing professionally. This kind of environment leads to higher

levels of engagement, creativity, and job satisfaction.

Leading Through Change

Change can be unsettling, and it's a leader's job to guide their team through uncertain times. Leaders with emotional intelligence can manage their own stress and help their team navigate change by being supportive, empathetic, and transparent. They're able to communicate clearly, manage emotions effectively, and maintain morale even in challenging situations.

Enhancing Team Performance

When leaders are emotionally intelligent, they're more attuned to the needs and motivations of their team members. This allows them to assign tasks that align with individuals' strengths and provide support where needed, which in turn boosts productivity and overall team performance.

HOW TO DEVELOP YOUR EMOTIONAL INTELLIGENCE

While some people may naturally have higher EQ than others, the good news is that emotional intelligence can be developed. By making a conscious effort to improve in the areas of self-awareness, self-regulation, empathy, motivation, and social skills, you can become a more emotionally intelligent leader. Here are some practical steps to help you get started:

Practice Self-Reflection
Make time each day to reflect on your emotions and how they've influenced your actions. Were there moments where you reacted out of anger, frustration, or fear? How did these emotions affect your decisions or interactions with others? By regularly reflecting on your emotional responses, you can become more aware of patterns and areas where you need to improve.

Seek Feedback
Sometimes, it's hard to see ourselves clearly. Ask for feedback from trusted colleagues or mentors about how you handle emotions and relationships. Be open to constructive criticism, and use it as an opportunity for growth.

Learn to Pause
When you're faced with a stressful or emotionally charged situation, practise the art of pausing before reacting. Take a deep

breath, give yourself a moment to process your emotions, and approach the situation with a calm and clear mind. This simple habit can prevent impulsive reactions and help you respond more thoughtfully.

Develop Empathy
To strengthen your empathy, practise active listening. When someone is speaking, focus on truly understanding their perspective without interrupting or preparing your response. Put yourself in their shoes, and respond in a way that acknowledges their emotions and concerns.

Work on Your Communication Skills
Being emotionally intelligent means being able to communicate effectively. Focus on improving your communication by being clear, direct, and respectful in your interactions. Pay attention to non-verbal cues like body language, tone of voice, and facial expressions, as these often communicate more than words.

Manage Stress
High stress can lower your EQ and make it harder to regulate your emotions. Develop healthy habits for managing stress, such as regular exercise, mindfulness practices, or simply taking time to relax. The more in control you are of your own stress levels, the better you'll be at handling challenging situations with emotional intelligence.

HOMEWORK: DEVELOPING YOUR EMOTIONAL INTELLIGENCE

Reflect on Your Emotions
Over the next week, keep a daily journal where you record moments when you experienced strong emotions at work. Write down what happened, how you felt, how you reacted, and what you could have done differently. Look for patterns and areas where you can improve.

Practice Empathy
In your next meeting or conversation, focus on listening more than you speak. Make it a point to fully understand the other person's perspective before responding. Afterward, reflect on how this changed the dynamic of the conversation.

Improve Self-Regulation
The next time you feel stressed or frustrated, try the "pause" technique. Take a moment to breathe and think before reacting. Write down how this impacted the outcome of the situation.

Ask for Feedback
Ask two or three trusted colleagues or team members to give you feedback on how you handle emotions and relationships in the workplace. Use their input to identify specific areas where you can

SNEHAMUMTAZ

improve.

CHAPTER 3: BUILDING TRUST AND CREDIBILITY

Trust and credibility are the cornerstones of effective leadership. Without them, even the most talented and knowledgeable leader will struggle to gain the support and loyalty of their team. Trust is not something that can be demanded or assumed—it must be earned, nurtured, and maintained over time. Credibility, on the other hand, is about proving your worth as a leader through your actions, expertise, and consistency.

In this chapter, we'll explore why trust and credibility are essential for leadership, how they can be built, and the steps you can take to cultivate these qualities in your leadership style. The goal is to help you understand that leadership is not just about managing tasks or making decisions; it's about creating meaningful relationships where people believe in you and feel safe under your guidance.

WHY TRUST AND CREDIBILITY MATTER IN LEADERSHIP

Leadership without trust is like building a house on a weak foundation—it will eventually crumble. Trust is what allows your team to follow your lead without fear of betrayal or doubt. It is what enables open communication, fosters collaboration, and encourages people to take risks, knowing that they are supported.

Credibility is closely tied to trust, but it's more about whether your team sees you as competent and reliable. A leader with credibility is someone who people believe can guide them through challenges, make fair decisions, and follow through on promises. Without credibility, your words and actions lose their impact.

Here are some key reasons why trust and credibility are critical for leadership:

Strengthening Relationships
Trust creates a bond between leaders and their teams. When your team trusts you, they are more likely to be open, honest, and collaborative. This leads to stronger relationships, better communication, and a more unified work environment. A leader who is trusted by their team can navigate conflicts more effectively and create a culture of support and loyalty.

Improving Team Morale
When people trust their leader, they feel secure and valued.

This sense of security boosts morale and encourages a positive attitude among team members. High morale leads to increased engagement, motivation, and a willingness to go the extra mile for the collective success of the team.

Facilitating Innovation and Risk-Taking
In any organisation, innovation requires a certain amount of risk. When team members trust their leader, they are more willing to take those risks because they know they will be supported, even if things don't go as planned. A trustworthy leader creates an environment where people feel comfortable thinking outside the box and experimenting with new ideas.

Enhancing Decision-Making
Credibility ensures that when a leader makes decisions, their team trusts that those decisions are well thought out, fair, and in the best interest of everyone involved. This reduces second-guessing and hesitation, allowing the team to act swiftly and confidently. A credible leader also gains the benefit of honest feedback from their team, as people feel safe to express their opinions without fear of retribution.

Building Long-Term Success
Leaders who prioritise trust and credibility create long-lasting success. Teams led by such leaders are more likely to remain loyal, reducing turnover and fostering a sense of community. Moreover, credibility ensures that the leader can weather difficult times without losing the respect and support of their team. Over time, this builds a resilient, high-performing organisation.

HOW TO BUILD TRUST AS A LEADER

Trust doesn't come with a title—it must be earned through consistent, thoughtful actions. Here are some essential strategies for building trust with your team:

Be Transparent
One of the quickest ways to build trust is through transparency. Be open and honest with your team about what's happening in the organisation, your expectations, and any challenges that may arise. Even when delivering difficult news, honesty is always better than sugar coating or withholding information. When your team feels like you're not hiding anything from them, they'll be more likely to trust you.
Example: If the company is going through a rough financial patch, be upfront with your team about the situation and the steps being taken to improve it. Keeping them informed prevents rumours and builds trust because they know you are being honest with them.

Lead by Example
Trust is built through actions, not just words. If you want your team to follow you, you need to model the behaviour you expect from them. This means holding yourself to the same standards of integrity, accountability, and work ethic that you demand from others. People are more likely to trust a leader who "walks the talk."
Example: If you ask your team to put in extra effort to meet a tight

deadline, be willing to roll up your sleeves and work alongside them. Leading by example shows that you're not asking them to do anything you wouldn't do yourself.

Show Consistency
Trust is established when your team knows what to expect from you. If you're inconsistent—one day approachable and supportive, the next distant and irritable—it's hard for people to trust you. Consistency in your behaviour, decision-making, and communication creates a sense of stability, which is key for building trust.
Example: If you make a commitment to offer feedback to your team every Friday, make sure you follow through consistently. Inconsistencies in your promises erode trust quickly.

Keep Your Promises
A broken promise, no matter how small, can quickly damage trust. If you commit to something, whether it's a deadline, a promotion, or a decision, make sure you deliver. If unforeseen circumstances prevent you from keeping a promise, communicate that openly and work to make things right.
Example: If you promise an employee that they'll be considered for a leadership role after completing a project, make sure you follow through when the time comes. Failing to do so will make them question your integrity and trustworthiness.

Be Accountable
A leader who blames others when things go wrong erodes trust. Taking responsibility for your mistakes and showing a willingness to learn from them demonstrates humility and accountability. When your team sees that you're willing to own up to your actions, they'll be more likely to do the same, creating a culture of trust and accountability.
Example: If a project you led didn't go as planned, take responsibility for any missteps and acknowledge what you could have done differently. This level of accountability shows your team that you value honesty and growth.

HOW TO BUILD CREDIBILITY AS A LEADER

While trust is about personal relationships, credibility is about your professional reputation. Credibility is built when your team sees that you have the knowledge, skills, and experience to lead them effectively. Here's how you can build and maintain your credibility:

Be Competent
Credibility starts with competence. You need to demonstrate that you know what you're doing. This doesn't mean you have to be an expert in every area, but you should have a solid understanding of the work your team is doing and stay informed about industry trends, challenges, and best practices. Continually improving your skills and knowledge shows your team that you're committed to being the best leader you can be.
Example: If you're leading a marketing team, stay up-to-date on the latest digital marketing trends and tools. When your team sees that you have the skills and knowledge to guide them, they'll be more confident in your leadership.

Be Fair and Objective
Credibility is built when your team sees that you're fair and objective in your decision-making. Favouritism, bias, or inconsistent treatment can quickly undermine your credibility. Strive to make decisions based on facts and what's best for the

team or organisation as a whole.

Example: If two team members are vying for a promotion, base your decision on their performance, qualifications, and potential, rather than personal preference. Your team will respect you more if they see that you're making decisions fairly.

Communicate Clearly

Clear communication is essential for credibility. When your team understands your vision, expectations, and decisions, they're more likely to trust your judgement. Be clear, concise, and open in your communication, and don't shy away from addressing difficult topics.

Example: When explaining a new strategy or direction, make sure your team fully understands why the change is happening and how it will benefit the organisation. Clarity prevents confusion and builds confidence in your leadership.

Admit When You Don't Know

Leaders are not expected to have all the answers. In fact, pretending to know everything can damage your credibility. It's far better to admit when you don't know something and commit to finding the answer than to bluff your way through a conversation. This honesty actually enhances your credibility because it shows that you're humble and willing to learn.

Example: If your team asks you a technical question you don't know the answer to, say, "I'm not sure, but I'll find out." This humility builds trust and shows that you're committed to accuracy.

Deliver Results

Ultimately, credibility is built through results. If you consistently deliver on your promises and lead your team to success, your credibility will naturally grow. Make sure you're setting realistic goals, meeting deadlines, and achieving the outcomes you've committed to.

Example: If you promise to increase sales by 10% within the next quarter, make sure you have a plan in place to achieve that goal.

When your team sees that you can deliver results, they'll have more confidence in your leadership.

HOMEWORK: STRENGTHENING TRUST AND CREDIBILITY

Build Trust through Transparency
Identify one area where you can be more transparent with your team. This could be about a current project, organisational changes, or expectations. Take action this week to openly communicate this information with your team and observe their response.

Lead by Example
Think about a situation where you can set a stronger example for your team. Whether it's working late on an important project or demonstrating a positive attitude during a challenging time, show your team that you're willing to practise what you preach.

Increase Your Credibility
Identify one area of your professional knowledge or skills that you could improve. Commit to reading an article, attending a workshop, or speaking with a mentor to deepen your understanding. Share this newfound knowledge with your team to demonstrate your ongoing commitment to growth.

Deliver on a Promise
Make a small promise to your team this week—something realistic

and attainable. It could be as simple as a commitment to provide feedback or complete a task by a certain deadline. Follow through on that promise to reinforce your reliability.

CHAPTER 4: MASTERING COMMUNICATION SKILLS FOR LEADERS

Communication is the lifeblood of leadership. Every leader, no matter their style, must communicate effectively to inspire, guide, and connect with their team. Yet, communication is often taken for granted, or worse, assumed to be something that happens naturally. The truth is, mastering communication takes intention, practice, and skill.

Good communication is not just about speaking clearly—it's about understanding your audience, listening actively, and delivering messages in a way that resonates. Whether it's leading a team meeting, handling a difficult conversation, or motivating your staff, how you communicate can make or break your leadership effectiveness.

In this chapter, we will explore the essential communication skills every leader needs to develop, how to adjust your communication style to different situations, and how to ensure your message is understood and acted upon. By mastering these skills, you'll be better equipped to build strong relationships, foster collaboration, and inspire your team to achieve their best.

THE IMPORTANCE OF COMMUNICATION IN LEADERSHIP

At its core, leadership is about getting people to move in the same direction to achieve a common goal. Without clear communication, this coordination is impossible. A leader might have great ideas, but if they can't articulate them well, those ideas will never see the light of day. Similarly, if a leader doesn't listen effectively, they may miss out on crucial feedback or insights from their team.

Here's why communication is so vital in leadership:

Aligning the Team
One of the primary roles of a leader is to ensure that everyone on the team is aligned with the organisation's vision, goals, and strategy. Clear communication ensures that everyone understands their roles and how their work contributes to the bigger picture. Without this alignment, team members may pull in different directions, leading to confusion and inefficiency.

Motivating and Inspiring
Leaders must also be able to inspire and motivate their teams. Great communication allows leaders to connect emotionally with their team, share the vision, and explain the "why" behind the work. A leader who communicates effectively can inspire loyalty, boost morale, and encourage people to go above and beyond.

Building Relationships

Strong relationships are built on trust and understanding, and communication is key to both. By communicating openly and honestly with your team, you create a culture where people feel valued, heard, and supported. This fosters stronger relationships and promotes teamwork and collaboration.

Handling Conflict

Conflicts are inevitable in any organisation, but good communication can help resolve them before they escalate. Leaders who can listen to all sides, communicate clearly, and facilitate constructive dialogue can mediate conflicts and find solutions that benefit the entire team.

Making Decisions

Leaders often need to make tough decisions, and those decisions need to be communicated in a way that's clear, concise, and respectful. Effective communication ensures that even if people don't agree with the decision, they understand why it was made and can respect the process.

KEY COMMUNICATION SKILLS EVERY LEADER NEEDS

Effective communication in leadership involves a combination of skills. It's not just about speaking; it's about connecting, listening, observing, and adjusting. Here are the core communication skills that every leader should strive to master:

Active Listening
Many people think of communication as primarily about talking, but great leaders know that listening is just as important—if not more so. Active listening involves fully focusing on the speaker, understanding their message, responding thoughtfully, and remembering what was said. It's about creating a space where people feel heard and understood.

How to Improve Active Listening:

Maintain eye contact to show engagement.

Avoid interrupting or jumping to conclusions before the speaker finishes.

Paraphrase or summarise what the speaker said to ensure clarity and show understanding.

Ask follow-up questions to dive deeper and show genuine interest.

Active listening not only helps leaders gather crucial information, but it also strengthens relationships. When your team feels heard, they are more likely to trust you, respect you, and follow your lead.

Clarity and Simplicity

The ability to communicate complex ideas in a clear, concise way is a hallmark of effective leadership. Overloading your team with jargon, lengthy explanations, or unclear instructions can lead to confusion and frustration. Instead, aim for simplicity. Strip away unnecessary details and focus on the key points you need to convey.

How to Communicate Clearly:

Organise your thoughts before speaking. Know what message you want to get across and stay on topic.

Use plain language. Avoid jargon unless you're sure your audience understands it.

Break down complex ideas into simpler parts and explain them step by step.

Summarise key takeaways at the end of your message to ensure understanding.

Clarity ensures that your team knows exactly what you want them to do, why it matters, and how they can succeed.

Empathy and Emotional Intelligence

As we explored in the previous chapter, emotional intelligence (EQ) is essential for leadership. In communication, EQ plays a crucial role in helping leaders connect with their teams on a deeper level. Empathy allows leaders to understand the emotions and perspectives of others, which can help them tailor their communication for different situations.

How to Communicate with Empathy:

Be aware of your team's emotional state. If you notice that someone seems stressed, ask how they're doing before diving into work discussions.

Use empathetic language. Phrases like "I understand how you feel" or "I can see why this is challenging" show that you care about your team's experiences.

Be mindful of tone and body language. Sometimes what's not said is just as important as what is. Your facial expressions, gestures, and tone of voice can greatly impact how your message is received.

By communicating with empathy, you foster a supportive environment where team members feel safe and understood.

Nonverbal Communication

Nonverbal communication—such as body language, facial expressions, and tone of voice—can often communicate more than words alone. Leaders who are aware of their nonverbal cues can reinforce their messages and ensure they are perceived as genuine and trustworthy.

How to Use Nonverbal Communication Effectively:

Maintain open, confident body language (e.g., stand tall, avoid crossing your arms).

Use facial expressions that match your message. Smiling when giving praise, for example, reinforces positivity.

Be mindful of your tone of voice. A calm, steady tone conveys confidence, while an overly harsh or sarcastic tone can undermine your message.

By aligning your nonverbal communication with your verbal message, you ensure that your team gets a consistent and authentic message.

Adaptability

Great communicators know how to adjust their communication style based on the audience and the situation. Not everyone on your team communicates in the same way. Some may prefer detailed explanations, while others appreciate quick, bullet-point summaries. Some may need face-to-face conversations, while others do better with written communication.

How to Adapt Your Communication Style:

Get to know your team's communication preferences. Do they prefer email, Slack, or in-person meetings? Tailor your approach accordingly.

Adjust your tone and message based on the context. For example, when discussing sensitive topics, a more gentle and empathetic approach is usually best, while a direct and confident approach is effective for rallying the team during a crisis.

Be flexible. If you notice that your team isn't responding well to your communication style, be willing to try new approaches until you find what works.

Adaptability ensures that your message resonates with each individual, improving both understanding and engagement.

Constructive Feedback
Leaders must be able to give feedback in a way that encourages growth rather than discouragement. Constructive feedback is clear, specific, and focused on behaviours rather than personal attributes. It provides the recipient with actionable steps they can take to improve, without making them feel defensive or undervalued.

How to Give Constructive Feedback:

Focus on the behaviour, not the person. For example, instead of saying "You're always late," say, "I've noticed that you've been late to several meetings."

Be specific. Instead of vague comments like "You need to improve," provide concrete examples and suggestions for improvement.

Balance positive and negative feedback. Acknowledge what the person is doing well before addressing areas for improvement.

End with encouragement. Make sure the person knows you believe in their ability to improve and succeed.

By giving constructive feedback, you help your team members grow and develop without diminishing their confidence or motivation.

COMMON COMMUNICATION CHALLENGES FOR LEADERS

Even with strong communication skills, leaders can face obstacles that make effective communication difficult. Understanding these challenges can help you navigate them more easily:

Information Overload
In today's fast-paced world, it's easy for team members to feel overwhelmed by the sheer volume of information they receive. As a leader, you need to be mindful of this and avoid contributing to the overload. Focus on delivering clear, concise messages that cut through the noise.

Miscommunication
Miscommunication happens when the message sent is not the message received. This can occur due to unclear language, cultural differences, or assumptions made by both the sender and receiver. To prevent miscommunication, ask for feedback to ensure your message was understood correctly.

Emotional Barriers
Sometimes emotions—both yours and your team's—can get in the way of effective communication. If someone is feeling stressed, frustrated, or defensive, they may not be able to fully engage with

the conversation. As a leader, it's important to be aware of these emotional barriers and address them before diving into important discussions.

HOMEWORK: BUILDING YOUR COMMUNICATION SKILLS

Active Listening Practice
Choose one meeting this week where you will consciously practise active listening. Focus on maintaining eye contact, not interrupting, and paraphrasing key points back to the speaker. Reflect afterward on how this changed the conversation dynamic.

Clarity Exercise
Take a recent email or presentation you've given and edit it for clarity. Remove any jargon, shorten long sentences, and focus on delivering your message in the simplest terms possible. Share the revised version with a colleague and ask for feedback.

Nonverbal Awareness
For one day, pay close attention to your nonverbal communication. Notice your body language, facial expressions, and tone of voice in various interactions. Are they aligned with the message you're trying to convey? Make adjustments as necessary and observe how people respond.

Giving Constructive Feedback
Identify one person on your team who could benefit from constructive feedback. Plan how you will deliver this feedback

using the principles outlined above. Focus on being specific, actionable, and balanced in your approach. After giving the feedback, reflect on how it was received and how you can continue improving this skill.

CHAPTER 5: DECISION MAKING AND PROBLEM SOLVING AS A LEADER

Leadership is not just about inspiring others, communicating effectively, or building trust—it's also about making decisions. Every day, leaders face choices that range from small operational details to strategic moves that can alter the direction of an organisation. How a leader approaches decision-making and problem-solving can significantly impact the success of their team, the well-being of employees, and the organisation's overall performance.

The ability to make sound decisions under pressure is a critical leadership skill. In a fast-paced world where information is constantly changing, leaders must be able to assess situations, weigh their options, and act with confidence. But decision-making is not just about speed—it's about making choices that are thoughtful, informed, and aligned with the goals of the organisation.

In this chapter, we will explore what it means to make decisions as a leader, how to approach problem-solving with confidence, and strategies to improve both. We will also discuss common pitfalls leaders face when making decisions and how to avoid them.

THE ROLE OF DECISION MAKING IN LEADERSHIP

Decisions are the essence of leadership. Whether it's choosing which direction to take, which initiatives to prioritise, or how to handle a crisis, leaders are constantly making decisions. The weight of these decisions can vary, but each one has an impact on the organisation and its people.

A leader's decision-making process is often what separates great leaders from mediocre ones. Good leaders can make tough decisions confidently and efficiently, even when faced with uncertainty. They are able to balance short-term needs with long-term objectives, consider different perspectives, and act in the best interest of their team and organisation.

There are three key areas where decision-making plays a vital role in leadership:

Strategic Decisions
These decisions shape the direction and future of the organisation. They are high-stakes and often involve long-term goals, such as entering new markets, launching new products, or restructuring teams. Strategic decisions require deep thinking, analysis, and careful consideration of the broader impact.

Operational Decisions
These are the day-to-day decisions that keep an organisation

running smoothly. They may involve how to allocate resources, manage workloads, or solve immediate problems. While operational decisions may seem less significant than strategic ones, they are crucial for ensuring efficiency and maintaining team morale.

Crisis Decisions

In times of crisis, leaders must act quickly and decisively. Whether it's a sudden market change, a public relations issue, or an internal conflict, crisis decision-making requires leaders to stay calm, assess the situation, and make swift yet informed choices. Crisis decisions can define a leader's reputation and impact the long-term trust within the organisation.

THE DECISION-MAKING PROCESS

Effective decision-making isn't a single action—it's a process. A good leader doesn't just jump to conclusions or make decisions based on gut feelings. Instead, they follow a structured approach that involves gathering information, analysing options, and considering the consequences.

Here's a step-by-step guide to the decision-making process:

Identify the Problem
The first step in any decision-making process is to clearly define the problem or challenge at hand. This might sound simple, but it's often where leaders can go wrong. If the problem is not properly understood, the decision made may not address the root cause. A well-defined problem sets the stage for effective problem-solving.

Key Questions to Ask:

What exactly is the issue?

Why is this problem important?

Who is affected by this problem?

What is the desired outcome?

Gather Information
Once the problem is identified, the next step is to gather all relevant information. This may involve collecting data, consulting with stakeholders, or researching similar situations.

A thorough understanding of the situation ensures that the decision will be based on facts rather than assumptions.

Key Considerations:

Look for both quantitative and qualitative data.

Seek input from team members or experts who have experience with similar challenges.

Consider past decisions and outcomes to identify patterns.

Be open to different perspectives—what might you be missing?

Generate Options

After gathering information, it's time to brainstorm potential solutions. The more options you generate, the better positioned you are to make an informed decision. Don't limit yourself to the first solution that comes to mind—explore alternatives, and think creatively.

Key Questions to Ask:

What are the different ways we can solve this problem?

Are there unconventional solutions we haven't considered?

What resources do we have available to implement these options?

Evaluate the Options

Once you have a list of potential solutions, it's time to evaluate each one. This involves weighing the pros and cons, considering the potential risks and benefits, and understanding the implications of each option. A good leader considers both the short-term and long-term consequences of their choices.

Key Considerations:

How will each option impact the team and organisation?

What are the potential risks associated with each choice?

Does this option align with the organisation's goals and values?

How feasible is each option, considering time, budget, and resources?

Make the Decision

After evaluating the options, it's time to make the decision. This is where leaders must demonstrate confidence and decisiveness. Even after a careful analysis, there may be uncertainty—no decision comes with a 100% guarantee. Great leaders understand that indecision can be more damaging than making the wrong choice, so they commit to their decisions with clarity.

Key Considerations:

Trust your analysis, but also trust your instincts.

Don't let fear of making a wrong decision paralyse you.

Communicate your decision clearly to all stakeholders, ensuring everyone understands the rationale behind it.

Implement the Decision

A decision is only as good as its implementation. Once the decision is made, leaders must ensure that it is effectively communicated and executed. This may involve delegating tasks, setting deadlines, and monitoring progress to ensure the decision achieves the desired results.

Key Considerations:

Make sure all team members understand their roles and responsibilities.

Provide the necessary resources and support to ensure successful execution.

Monitor the situation and be prepared to make adjustments if needed.

Evaluate the Results

The final step in the decision-making process is to evaluate the results. Did the decision solve the problem? What were the outcomes? What can be learned from this experience? Reflection and evaluation help leaders refine their decision-making skills and improve future outcomes.

Key Questions to Ask:

Did the decision achieve the desired outcome?

What went well, and what could have been done better?

What lessons can be applied to future decisions?

COMMON PITFALLS IN DECISION MAKING

Even the most experienced leaders can make mistakes in their decision-making process. Understanding these common pitfalls can help you avoid them and make more effective decisions:

Analysis Paralysis
Sometimes leaders become so focused on gathering information and analysing options that they never actually make a decision. This is known as analysis paralysis. While it's important to be thorough, leaders must also recognize when it's time to act.
How to Avoid It:
Set a deadline for making the decision and stick to it. Trust that you've gathered enough information to make an informed choice, and don't let fear of uncertainty hold you back.

Overconfidence
On the opposite end of the spectrum is overconfidence. Some leaders rush into decisions without fully considering the consequences, believing they can handle whatever comes their way. While confidence is important, overconfidence can lead to poor decision-making.
How to Avoid It:
Take time to reflect on your decision-making process. Ask for feedback from trusted colleagues or advisors, and be open to the possibility that your initial instinct might not always be right.

Ignoring Feedback
Leaders who are unwilling to listen to feedback from their team or

colleagues may miss out on valuable insights that could improve their decision-making. It's important to involve others in the process and remain open to different perspectives.

How to Avoid It:

Actively seek out feedback during the information-gathering phase. Encourage open dialogue and be willing to adjust your decision based on new information.

Emotional Bias

Emotions can cloud judgement, especially in high-stress situations. Leaders who allow their emotions to dictate their decisions may act impulsively or make choices that are not in the best interest of the organisation.

How to Avoid It:

Practise emotional intelligence by recognizing when your emotions are influencing your decision-making. Take a step back, breathe, and consider the situation from a more objective perspective.

PROBLEM SOLVING AS A LEADER

Decision-making and problem-solving go hand in hand. Leaders are often called upon to solve problems, whether they are related to team dynamics, operational challenges, or external factors. Problem-solving is about identifying the root cause of an issue, developing solutions, and taking action to resolve it.

There are several problem-solving techniques that leaders can use:

Root Cause Analysis
Root cause analysis is a method used to identify the underlying cause of a problem. Instead of focusing on symptoms, this approach digs deeper to uncover the true issue. For example, if a project is delayed, the root cause might not be poor time management—it could be a lack of resources or unclear expectations.

Key Steps:

Define the problem clearly.

Ask "why" multiple times to identify the root cause.

Once the root cause is identified, develop solutions that address the core issue.

SWOT Analysis
SWOT (Strengths, Weaknesses, Opportunities, and Threats) analysis is a tool that helps leaders assess the internal and external factors affecting a problem. By understanding the

strengths and weaknesses within the organisation, as well as external opportunities and threats, leaders can develop a more comprehensive solution.

Key Steps:

Identify the strengths, weaknesses, opportunities, and threats related to the problem.

Prioritise the factors that have the most significant impact.

Develop strategies to leverage strengths and opportunities while mitigating weaknesses and threats.

Brainstorming

Brainstorming is a creative problem-solving technique that involves generating as many ideas as possible without judgement. This approach encourages team collaboration and can lead to innovative solutions that might not have been considered otherwise.

Key Steps:

Set a clear goal for the brainstorming session.

Encourage participants to share ideas freely without criticism.

Evaluate the ideas after the session and select the most viable solutions.

Mind Mapping

Mind mapping is a visual problem-solving tool that helps leaders organise their thoughts and ideas. By creating a visual representation of the problem and potential solutions, leaders can see connections between different elements and develop a more holistic approach.

Key Steps:

Start with the central problem in the middle of the map.

Branch out with related ideas, solutions, or factors influencing the problem.

Use colours, symbols, and images to make the mind map more

engaging and easier to understand.

HOMEWORK: IMPROVING YOUR DECISION-MAKING AND PROBLEM-SOLVING SKILLS

Reflection on Past Decisions
Think of a significant decision you've made in the past six months. Reflect on the process you used to make that decision. Did you follow a structured approach, or was it more instinctive? What was the outcome? What could you have done differently? Write down your reflections and consider how you can improve your decision-making process in the future.

Scenario Planning
Choose a hypothetical scenario relevant to your current role, such as a sudden budget cut or a team conflict. Outline the decision-making steps you would take to address the situation. Consider gathering information, generating options, evaluating risks, and implementing your decision. Share your plan with a colleague or mentor for feedback.

Problem-Solving Exercise
Identify a current challenge or problem you are facing at work. Use one of the problem-solving techniques discussed in this

chapter (such as root cause analysis or brainstorming) to develop a solution. Document your process and evaluate the results after implementing your solution.

CHAPTER 6: LEADING THROUGH CHANGE AND UNCERTAINTY

Change is one of the few constants in life, and it's certainly an ever-present factor in leadership. Whether it's adapting to new market conditions, organisational restructuring, technological advancements, or global events, leaders are frequently called upon to guide their teams through periods of change and uncertainty.

Leading through change is challenging because it often involves unpredictability, discomfort, and resistance from team members who may feel unsettled by the unknown. However, great leaders understand that change is an opportunity for growth, innovation, and improvement. When managed effectively, transitions can strengthen a team's resilience and pave the way for future success.

In this chapter, we will explore how to lead through change with confidence, support your team during uncertain times, and foster an environment where people can adapt and thrive despite the challenges. Leading through change requires not only strategy but also empathy, communication, and an ability to stay calm under pressure.

UNDERSTANDING CHANGE AND WHY IT'S HARD

Change can be daunting for everyone. As humans, we tend to find comfort in routine and familiarity, so when things shift—whether that's in our personal lives or within the workplace—it often triggers anxiety, fear, or resistance. These emotions are natural responses to uncertainty because we fear losing control or moving into the unknown.

Here are a few reasons why change is particularly challenging for teams and individuals:

Loss of Control
When change occurs, people often feel like they've lost control over their environment or their roles. This can lead to a sense of helplessness, which in turn can breed fear and resistance. People worry about how change will affect them personally—will they lose their job, their status, or their responsibilities?

Fear of the Unknown
The uncertainty that accompanies change can create stress. People tend to worry about what they don't know. "What will happen next?" "How will this impact me and my work?" When the future is unclear, it's natural for individuals to feel anxious.

Comfort in Routine
Many individuals grow attached to their daily routines and

established workflows. Even if these routines aren't the most efficient or beneficial, they provide a sense of stability. Change disrupts this comfort zone, and adapting to new ways of doing things takes effort and mental energy.

Potential for Failure

Change brings with it the risk of failure. Whether it's implementing new systems or taking on new responsibilities, people fear that they may not be able to succeed in an unfamiliar environment. This fear can lead to resistance or reluctance to embrace the changes.

THE ROLE OF A LEADER DURING CHANGE

As a leader, it is your responsibility to guide your team through change and help them navigate uncertainty. Your role is not only to communicate the practical steps of the transition but also to provide emotional support, foster trust, and lead by example. Here's how you can do that:

Be a Stabilising Force
During periods of uncertainty, your team will look to you for stability and reassurance. It's important to project calm and confidence, even when the situation is evolving. If you appear stressed or uncertain, it can heighten the anxiety of your team. On the other hand, if you remain steady, your team is more likely to feel secure and trust that things will be okay.

Key Takeaway:

Be mindful of your demeanour. Even in challenging situations, focus on what you can control, and keep a positive, solution-oriented mindset. Your attitude will set the tone for the rest of the team.

Communicate Openly and Honestly
Clear, transparent communication is critical during times of change. People are more likely to resist change if they don't understand what's happening or why it's necessary. As a leader,

it's your job to explain the reasons behind the change, how it will affect the team, and what the benefits will be in the long term.
Key Takeaway:

Be open and honest in your communication. Share as much information as you can about the situation, and encourage your team to ask questions. Address their concerns and be transparent about any uncertainties.

Empathise with Your Team
Empathy is one of the most important qualities a leader can demonstrate during periods of change. Recognize that people are likely feeling a range of emotions, from anxiety to frustration to excitement. Show that you understand their concerns and are there to support them through the transition.
Key Takeaway:

Take time to listen to your team members individually. Ask how they're feeling and offer reassurance where needed. Make it clear that you value their well-being, and let them know you're available to help them navigate challenges.

Foster Adaptability
Change is inevitable, so helping your team become more adaptable is a long-term strategy that will benefit both them and the organisation. Encourage a culture of learning and experimentation, where team members feel comfortable trying new approaches without fear of failure.
Key Takeaway:

Emphasise the importance of adaptability as a skill. Reward efforts to embrace new ways of working, and celebrate small wins during the transition. By fostering a mindset of flexibility, you can make future changes easier to manage.

STRATEGIES FOR LEADING THROUGH CHANGE

Now that we've established the importance of communication, empathy, and adaptability, let's dive into specific strategies for leading through change. These practical tips will help you guide your team more effectively during transitions:

Paint a Clear Vision for the Future
One of the best ways to reduce uncertainty is to provide a clear vision of where the change is leading. If your team understands the long-term benefits of the change, they'll be more likely to buy into it. Articulate the goals and outcomes of the change, and explain how it aligns with the organisation's broader mission.

Key Action:

When announcing a change, start by sharing the vision. Explain why the change is necessary, how it will improve things for the organisation, and how the team will be better off in the future.

Break Down the Transition into Manageable Steps
Change can feel overwhelming, especially if it's large-scale or complex. Help your team manage this by breaking the transition down into smaller, manageable steps. Provide a roadmap of what will happen and when, and set clear milestones for progress.

Key Action:

Create a detailed timeline or plan for the change, and share it with your team. Outline the key steps involved, who is responsible for each, and what the expected outcomes are. This will give your team a sense of structure and help them feel more in control.

Involve Your Team in the Process

People are more likely to embrace change if they feel they have a say in it. Whenever possible, involve your team in the decision-making process. Ask for their input, ideas, and feedback, and encourage them to take ownership of the transition.

Key Action:

Hold team meetings or workshops to brainstorm how the team can best adapt to the changes. Listen to their concerns and suggestions, and incorporate their feedback into the overall plan.

Provide Support and Resources

Change often requires new skills, tools, or approaches. Make sure your team has the support and resources they need to succeed. This might involve providing training, adjusting workloads, or offering additional support to those who are struggling to adapt.

Key Action:

Assess what resources your team will need to thrive during the transition. Whether it's new software, training sessions, or extra time to adjust, ensure that everyone has what they need to succeed.

Monitor Progress and Be Flexible

As the change progresses, keep an eye on how your team is doing. Are there any roadblocks? Is the transition going as planned? Be flexible enough to adjust your approach if needed. Remember, change rarely happens smoothly, so be prepared to make adjustments along the way.

Key Action:

Regularly check in with your team to assess progress. Ask how things are going, and be willing to tweak the plan if necessary. Flexibility is key to making the transition as smooth as possible.

LEADING THROUGH UNCERTAINTY

Change and uncertainty often go hand in hand. While change can be planned and structured, uncertainty is less predictable. Leading through uncertainty is perhaps one of the most challenging aspects of leadership, but it's also where true leaders shine.

Uncertainty can come from external factors like economic downturns, global events, or market disruptions, or from internal challenges like a lack of information or sudden leadership changes. During uncertain times, leaders must navigate ambiguity, keep their team grounded, and continue to drive progress, even when the future is unclear.

Here's how you can lead effectively through uncertainty:

Accept That You Don't Have All the Answers
As a leader, it's important to acknowledge that you won't always have all the answers. During uncertain times, it's okay to admit that some things are out of your control or that you're still figuring things out. Being transparent about the situation can build trust with your team.

Key Takeaway:

Share what you know with your team, and be honest about what remains uncertain. Rather than trying to appear in control of everything, focus on what you can control and lead with integrity.

Stay Grounded and Focus on What You Can Control

When the future is uncertain, it's easy to get caught up in worrying about what might happen. However, as a leader, your job is to keep your team grounded. Encourage your team to focus on the tasks and decisions within their control, and guide them through the things they can influence.

Key Takeaway:

Help your team break down large, uncertain challenges into smaller, actionable tasks. Encourage them to focus on what they can achieve today rather than worrying about what's out of their control.

Be Visible and Present

During times of uncertainty, it's essential to be visible and present for your team. Regular check-ins, even if brief, can go a long way in providing reassurance and keeping communication open. Let your team know that you're there for them and that they're not alone in navigating the situation.

Key Takeaway:

Make yourself available to your team. Hold regular team meetings and one-on-ones to check in on how they're doing. Show empathy, provide guidance, and be a consistent presence, even when times are tough.

HOMEWORK: BUILDING RESILIENCE IN TIMES OF CHANGE

Reflect on a Major Change
Think about a significant change you've experienced in your career or personal life. How did you handle it? What were the emotions you went through? How did you eventually adapt? Write down your reflections and consider what you've learned about yourself in the process.

Adaptability Practice
Identify an area of your work where you tend to resist change. It could be a certain workflow, tool, or process. Over the next week, challenge yourself to approach it with a more open, adaptable mindset. Experiment with new ways of doing things, and reflect on how it feels to step outside your comfort zone.

Create a Vision for a Hypothetical Change
Imagine a significant change that might occur within your organisation, such as a leadership transition or a new technology implementation. Write down a vision for how you would lead your team through this change. What steps would you take? How would you communicate the vision? Share your plan with a colleague for feedback.

CHAPTER 7: MOTIVATING AND INSPIRING YOUR TEAM

Motivating and inspiring your team is at the heart of great leadership. A leader who can unlock the full potential of their team by encouraging passion, dedication, and creativity sets the foundation for long-term success. But motivating a group of individuals—each with unique personalities, aspirations, and challenges—is not a one-size-fits-all task. It requires understanding what drives each person, creating a shared sense of purpose, and leading by example.

In this chapter, we'll explore how you can tap into the unique motivators of your team, foster an environment that encourages inspiration and engagement, and cultivate a culture where people feel empowered to do their best work.

THE DIFFERENCE BETWEEN MOTIVATION AND INSPIRATION

Before diving into specific strategies, it's essential to clarify the difference between motivation and inspiration. While the two terms are often used interchangeably, they play slightly different roles in leadership:

Motivation is about encouraging people to take action. It's what gets your team members moving toward their goals, whether through rewards, recognition, or personal satisfaction. Motivation can be internal (coming from within the individual) or external (driven by outside factors, like promotions or incentives).

Inspiration is more about lifting people's spirits and helping them see the bigger picture. It's not just about what needs to get done, but why it matters. Inspiration comes from a deeper sense of purpose, meaning, or vision, and it often results in long-lasting commitment and passion.

As a leader, your role is to not only motivate your team to meet their targets but also inspire them to feel genuinely connected to their work and excited about the collective goals. While motivation might light the fire, inspiration keeps it burning.

UNDERSTANDING WHAT DRIVES YOUR TEAM

Motivating your team starts with understanding that each person is driven by different factors. For one team member, recognition might be the key motivator, while another might be driven by the opportunity for growth or a sense of accomplishment. Therefore, the first step in effective leadership is getting to know what drives each individual.

Identify Personal Motivators
To understand what motivates your team, you need to engage with them on a personal level. Take the time to have conversations with each team member about their goals, what excites them, and what they want to achieve. Ask questions like:

"What do you find most fulfilling about your work?"

"What are you hoping to achieve in the next year?"

"What can I do to help you feel more engaged and successful in your role?"

By understanding their personal motivators, you'll be better equipped to tailor your approach and provide the support and encouragement they need.

Internal vs. External Motivation
There are two types of motivation: internal and external. It's

crucial to recognize which one resonates most with each team member.

Internal Motivation: Some individuals are driven by intrinsic rewards, such as personal growth, mastery, autonomy, or a sense of purpose. These people thrive when they feel their work is meaningful and aligned with their values.

External Motivation: Others are more motivated by extrinsic rewards, such as bonuses, promotions, or public recognition. While external motivators can be effective, they tend to provide short-term boosts, while internal motivators often lead to deeper, long-lasting engagement.

As a leader, your goal is to strike a balance between these two types of motivation, leveraging external rewards when appropriate while fostering internal motivation to create a more sustainable sense of fulfilment.

CREATING A CULTURE OF PURPOSE AND MEANING

One of the most powerful ways to inspire your team is by helping them see how their work fits into a larger purpose. When people feel like they're contributing to something meaningful, they're more likely to feel passionate and engaged.

Define a Clear Vision
To inspire your team, it's essential to have a clear vision of where you're going as a leader and as an organisation. This vision should be compelling and easy to understand. It should also resonate on both an individual and a collective level, helping each team member understand how their contributions move the team or company closer to that vision.

For example, if your organisation is dedicated to making a positive impact on the environment, make sure your team understands how their specific roles contribute to that larger goal. When the bigger picture is clear, people are more likely to feel a sense of purpose in their daily tasks.

Connect Work to Individual Goals
People are more likely to stay motivated when they can see how their work aligns with their personal goals. As a leader, it's essential to help your team make these connections. For example, if you know a team member is motivated by learning new skills,

frame new tasks or projects as opportunities for growth.

During regular check-ins, discuss how their current responsibilities are helping them move closer to their individual goals. When people see that their professional and personal aspirations are aligned, they're more likely to feel invested in their work.

STRATEGIES TO MOTIVATE AND INSPIRE YOUR TEAM

Now that we've covered the foundational elements of motivation and inspiration, let's look at specific strategies you can use to motivate and inspire your team in practical ways.

Provide Regular Recognition and Appreciation
One of the most straightforward yet effective ways to motivate your team is to recognize their efforts. Everyone likes to feel appreciated, and regular acknowledgment of your team's hard work goes a long way in keeping morale high.

Verbal Praise: Take time during team meetings or one-on-one sessions to verbally acknowledge individual contributions. Let team members know you've noticed their efforts and that their work matters.

Public Recognition: Recognize team members publicly, whether through shout-outs in team meetings, company-wide newsletters, or other forms of recognition that highlight their accomplishments.

Pro Tip: Be specific when giving recognition. Instead of saying, "Great job," highlight exactly what the person did that was exceptional. This reinforces the behaviours you want to see more of and makes the praise feel more genuine.

Encourage Ownership and Autonomy
When people feel empowered to make decisions and take ownership of their work, they're more likely to feel motivated and engaged. Giving your team the autonomy to manage their own projects fosters a sense of responsibility and pride.

Delegate Meaningfully: Instead of micromanaging, delegate projects and trust your team to handle them. Give them the authority to make decisions and come up with their own solutions.

Encourage Innovation: Create a culture where new ideas are welcomed and innovation is encouraged. When team members feel they have the freedom to experiment and try new things, they're more likely to stay engaged.

Create Opportunities for Growth

Many people are motivated by the opportunity to learn and grow. As a leader, you can help your team members stay motivated by providing them with opportunities to develop new skills, take on new responsibilities, or explore areas of interest.

Offer Learning Opportunities: Encourage continuous learning by providing access to training, workshops, or professional development resources.

Assign Challenging Projects: Challenge your team members with new and exciting projects that stretch their abilities. When people feel they're growing and progressing, they're more likely to stay motivated.

Foster a Positive Team Culture

A positive and supportive team environment is crucial for maintaining motivation. When people feel connected to their colleagues and enjoy coming to work, they're more likely to be engaged and committed.

Promote Collaboration: Encourage teamwork and collaboration by fostering a culture where team members help and support one another.

Celebrate Wins Together: Take time to celebrate both big and small wins as a team. Whether it's reaching a major milestone or completing a challenging project, celebrating together strengthens team bonds and reinforces a sense of shared purpose.

Be a Role Model

As a leader, your behaviour sets the tone for the entire team. If you're passionate, motivated, and committed, your team will likely mirror those qualities. On the other hand, if you're disengaged or negative, it can dampen the team's motivation.

Lead with Passion: Show your team that you're passionate about the work and committed to the organisation's vision. Your enthusiasm can be contagious.

Stay Positive: Even during challenging times, maintain a positive and solution-oriented attitude. Positivity in leadership encourages resilience and helps the team stay motivated, even when facing obstacles.

OVERCOMING COMMON MOTIVATION CHALLENGES

Even with the best intentions, leaders may encounter challenges when trying to motivate their teams. Here's how to overcome a few common obstacles:

Burnout
Burnout is a common challenge, especially in high-pressure environments. When team members are overworked or feel overwhelmed, their motivation can dwindle.

Solution: Prioritise well-being by encouraging work-life balance, offering flexible work arrangements, and regularly checking in on how your team is feeling. Be proactive in recognizing the signs of burnout and address them early.

Lack of Clear Direction
When team members don't understand the goals or expectations, they may feel lost or disengaged.

Solution: Make sure your team has clear goals, objectives, and deadlines. Regularly communicate the vision and keep your team focused on the bigger picture.

Resistance to Change

Change can be unsettling and lead to disengagement if not managed properly.

Solution: Involve your team in the decision-making process, explain the reasons behind the change, and provide support during transitions. People are more likely to stay motivated if they feel included and informed.

HOMEWORK: MOTIVATING YOUR TEAM IN ACTION

Personal Motivator Identification
Schedule one-on-one meetings with each of your team members to discuss their personal goals and what motivates them. After these discussions, create a personalised plan for each individual that helps align their work with their motivators.

Vision Mapping Exercise
Create a vision board or written map for your team's current projects. Include how each task contributes to the team's larger goals and purpose. Share this with your team during a meeting and discuss how everyone's efforts fit into the bigger picture.

Recognizing Successes
Start a weekly "success story" segment in your team meetings where you highlight an achievement or contribution from a team member. Be specific in your praise and encourage the rest of the team to join in recognizing their colleagues.

CHAPTER 8: DELEGATION AND EMPOWERMENT

Delegation and empowerment are two of the most vital skills any effective leader must master. While they are often discussed in the context of leadership, they are more than just management tactics—they are about building trust, fostering growth, and creating an environment where team members feel capable, valued, and motivated to take ownership of their work. Proper delegation is the art of assigning tasks to the right people, and empowerment is giving them the autonomy and support to succeed.

For many leaders, delegating can be challenging. It requires a balance of letting go of control while maintaining accountability, a skill that takes both practice and a mindset shift. But when done right, delegation leads to increased productivity, higher employee satisfaction, and a stronger, more capable team.

This chapter will guide you through the importance of delegation and how to delegate in a way that empowers your team, builds trust, and encourages growth, all while maintaining the integrity of your leadership.

WHY DELEGATION IS CRUCIAL FOR LEADERSHIP SUCCESS

As a leader, your time and energy are valuable and finite. You cannot—and should not—do everything yourself. Learning to delegate allows you to focus on strategic, high-level priorities while empowering your team to take on responsibilities and contribute to the organisation's success.

Increases Productivity and Efficiency
By delegating tasks, you free up time to focus on more critical areas where your leadership is needed, such as decision-making, strategy, and innovation. At the same time, delegation helps your team work more effectively by spreading the workload and ensuring that tasks are completed by those best suited for the job.

Think of it like a relay race: The fastest runners don't try to do the entire race themselves; they pass the baton to others who are also skilled runners. Similarly, delegation ensures that the right person handles the right task, increasing overall productivity.

Develops Your Team's Skills
Delegation is also a tool for growth. By delegating challenging tasks or responsibilities, you give your team members the opportunity to develop new skills, gain confidence, and grow professionally. They learn to take ownership of their work, which enhances their capabilities and strengthens the team as a whole.

When you delegate properly, you're not just shifting work off your plate—you're building the skills and confidence of your team members, which ultimately creates a stronger and more capable workforce.

Builds Trust and Accountability

Effective delegation fosters a sense of trust between you and your team. By entrusting someone with an important task, you show that you have confidence in their abilities. This trust encourages accountability, as team members are more likely to take ownership of their work when they know it's been entrusted to them with confidence.

Over time, this trust creates a positive feedback loop. As team members consistently deliver results, your confidence in them grows, and in turn, their confidence in themselves increases.

THE POWER OF EMPOWERMENT

While delegation is about assigning tasks, empowerment is about giving people the autonomy and support to complete those tasks successfully. Empowerment is not just about telling people what to do but enabling them to make decisions, solve problems, and take initiative without constant oversight.

Autonomy Boosts Engagement
When people feel empowered in their roles, they are more likely to be engaged and invested in their work. Empowerment creates a sense of ownership, where individuals feel responsible for their contributions and outcomes. When people are given the freedom to make decisions and take action, they're more likely to be passionate about their work and motivated to see it through.

Encourages Innovation and Creativity
Empowered employees often feel more comfortable thinking outside the box and coming up with innovative solutions. When individuals know they have the authority to experiment, they are more likely to propose new ideas, challenge the status quo, and offer creative solutions to problems. As a leader, encouraging this type of creative thinking is key to fostering innovation within your team.

Reduces Micromanagement and Increases Trust
Micromanagement stifles creativity and can lead to disengagement. Empowerment, on the other hand, reduces the need for constant oversight, freeing you as a leader

from the pressure to manage every detail. When your team feels empowered, they are more likely to step up and take initiative, allowing you to focus on bigger-picture leadership responsibilities.

HOW TO DELEGATE EFFECTIVELY

While delegation may seem simple, many leaders struggle with letting go of tasks or worry that others won't complete them as well as they would. However, effective delegation involves more than just assigning tasks; it's about ensuring that those tasks are set up for success.

Identify the Right Tasks to Delegate
Not every task should be delegated. As a leader, you should focus on delegating tasks that can be handled by others, while keeping responsibilities that require your specific expertise or insight. Consider delegating:

Routine tasks that don't require your direct involvement.

Tasks that are good learning opportunities for your team.

Responsibilities that can help develop someone's skills or confidence.

Keep the high-priority or complex tasks that only you, as the leader, should be handling, such as strategic decision-making or stakeholder management.

Choose the Right People
To delegate effectively, you need to assign tasks to the right people. Consider the strengths, skills, and workload of each team member when deciding who should take on a specific task. Ask yourself:

Who has the necessary skills to handle this task?

Who could benefit from the experience of completing this assignment?

Who has the capacity to take on additional work without becoming overwhelmed?

Matching the task with the right person increases the likelihood of success and helps your team members grow in the process.

Provide Clear Instructions and Expectations
Once you've identified the task and the right person to handle it, it's essential to provide clear instructions. Be specific about the goals, deadlines, and desired outcomes. Make sure the team member understands the task's importance and how it fits into the broader objectives of the team or organisation.

While it's important to give clear guidelines, avoid being overly prescriptive about how the work should be done. Allow your team members the freedom to approach the task in their own way, as long as the results meet your expectations.

Offer Support and Resources
Delegation doesn't mean abandoning your team members to figure everything out on their own. It's essential to offer support and provide the resources they need to complete the task successfully. This might include access to tools, training, or other team members for collaboration.

Let them know that you're available for guidance if needed, but be careful not to hover or micromanage. Trust that they can handle the task, and give them the space to prove it.

Follow Up and Provide Feedback
Delegation doesn't end when you hand off a task. Following up is critical to ensure that progress is being made and that any issues are addressed early on. Check in periodically to offer support and ask for updates without being overbearing.

Once the task is completed, provide constructive feedback. If the task was completed well, acknowledge the accomplishment and express appreciation. If there are areas for improvement, provide feedback in a way that helps the individual grow and learn from the experience.

EMPOWERMENT IN ACTION: PRACTICAL STEPS FOR LEADERS

Empowerment goes beyond delegation by instilling a sense of ownership and encouraging team members to take initiative. Here's how you can empower your team:

Encourage Decision-Making

Empowerment starts with encouraging your team to make decisions. When possible, let your team members take ownership of decisions within their roles. This helps them build confidence and develop critical thinking skills. Start by delegating smaller decisions and gradually increase the scope as their confidence grows.

Create a Safe Space for Failure

One of the key elements of empowerment is creating an environment where failure is seen as part of the learning process. Empowerment doesn't mean that mistakes won't happen—but it does mean creating a culture where people feel safe to take risks and learn from setbacks. Let your team know that you support their efforts, even when things don't go perfectly.

Recognize and Celebrate Initiative

When your team members take initiative, make sure to recognize and celebrate their efforts. Public recognition or simply acknowledging their proactive behaviour goes a long way in reinforcing a culture of empowerment. Highlighting success stories inspires others to step up and take ownership as well.

OVERCOMING DELEGATION AND EMPOWERMENT CHALLENGES

Even with the best intentions, delegation and empowerment can present challenges. Let's look at some common hurdles and how to overcome them.

Reluctance to Let Go
Some leaders hesitate to delegate because they fear losing control or believe that no one else can do the task as well as they can.

Solution: Start small by delegating less critical tasks, then gradually delegate more responsibilities as your confidence in your team grows. Remember, delegation isn't about perfection—it's about allowing others to grow and contribute.

Lack of Confidence in the Team
Leaders may feel their team lacks the necessary skills or experience to handle certain tasks.

Solution: View delegation as an opportunity for growth. Provide the necessary training or resources to help your team develop the skills they need. Trust takes time to build, but it starts with giving people the chance to prove themselves.

Fear of Failure

Empowerment can sometimes feel risky because it involves allowing others to make decisions or take risks.

Solution: Foster a culture where mistakes are seen as learning opportunities. Empower your team to experiment, but also provide support and guidance to minimise risk. Celebrate both successes and lessons learned from failures.

HOMEWORK: DELEGATION AND EMPOWERMENT IN PRACTICE

Delegation Assessment
Review your current workload and identify three tasks that you can delegate to your team. Assign these tasks based on your team members' skills and interests. Be clear in your instructions and follow up with feedback once the task is completed.

Empowerment in Action
Identify a decision or responsibility that you can empower a team member to take on. Allow them to take ownership of the task or decision-making process. Check in periodically to offer support, but let them take the lead.

Recognition and Celebration
Create a recognition system within your team where proactive behaviour and initiative are celebrated. Start by recognizing a team member who has recently taken initiative and share their story with the rest of the team.

CHAPTER 9: CONFLICT RESOLUTION AND DIFFICULT CONVERSATIONS

Conflict is an inevitable part of working with others. Whether it's a misunderstanding between colleagues, differing opinions on strategy, or personal issues affecting professional relationships, conflict will arise. As a leader, your ability to effectively manage and resolve conflict is critical to maintaining a healthy, productive team environment. How you handle conflict not only impacts the individuals involved but can also shape the overall culture of your organisation.

Difficult conversations, such as providing constructive criticism, addressing underperformance, or dealing with interpersonal issues, can be uncomfortable. However, avoiding or mishandling these conversations can lead to unresolved issues, resentment, and a breakdown in team morale.

This chapter will explore the importance of conflict resolution and how to approach difficult conversations with confidence, empathy, and effectiveness. Understanding these skills will help you foster a team culture where problems are addressed constructively, and people feel heard, respected, and supported.

THE NATURE OF CONFLICT IN LEADERSHIP

Conflict can feel negative, but it's important to recognize that it isn't always bad. In fact, conflict can be a sign of healthy debate, diversity of thought, and an opportunity for growth. When people with different perspectives come together, conflict can spark innovation and creative problem-solving.

However, not all conflicts are productive. Left unchecked, misunderstandings or interpersonal tensions can escalate, leading to resentment, poor communication, and reduced team performance. As a leader, your role is to navigate conflict in a way that transforms it from a barrier into an opportunity for dialogue and improvement.

Common Causes of Conflict

Before diving into conflict resolution, it's important to understand the root causes of conflict in the workplace. Identifying the underlying issues can help you address them more effectively.

Miscommunication
A significant amount of conflict stems from misunderstandings or poor communication. People may interpret messages differently, miss key information, or jump to conclusions, which can lead to disagreements or hurt feelings.

Differing Priorities or Goals
When team members have conflicting priorities, goals, or approaches to work, tension can arise. For example, one person might prioritise speed while another prioritises quality, leading to frustration over conflicting expectations.

Personality Clashes
Everyone has their own communication style, values, and way of working. Sometimes, these differences can cause friction between individuals. Personality clashes, while often not based on any specific event, can create ongoing tension if not addressed.

Power Dynamics
Conflicts often emerge when there are imbalances or struggles for power within a team. Someone may feel undervalued, ignored, or micromanaged, leading to frustration and tension.

Workload and Stress
High-pressure environments, heavy workloads, or tight deadlines can heighten emotions and lead to conflict. When people are stressed or overwhelmed, they may become more irritable or prone to conflict.

Understanding these common causes helps you as a leader to anticipate potential issues and address them before they escalate.

THE ROLE OF A LEADER IN CONFLICT RESOLUTION

As a leader, your responsibility in conflict situations is not to pick sides but to act as a mediator. You are there to facilitate a resolution that is fair, constructive, and helps the team move forward. Here's how you can approach conflict resolution effectively:

Remain Neutral and Objective
When conflicts arise, it's important to remain neutral. Avoid taking sides or letting personal biases influence your judgement. Your goal is to mediate the conflict and help the involved parties find common ground. By staying objective, you create an environment where both sides feel heard and respected.

Encourage Open Dialogue
Effective conflict resolution starts with communication. Encourage the parties involved to express their thoughts and feelings openly, without fear of judgement. Creating a safe space for open dialogue is key to understanding the root of the conflict and finding a path forward.

Focus on the Issue, Not the Person
Conflict resolution is about addressing the issue at hand, not attacking the people involved. Make sure that the conversation stays focused on the problem, rather than allowing it to become

personal. This helps to prevent emotions from escalating and keeps the discussion productive.

Be Empathetic
Approach conflict with empathy. Try to understand how the other person is feeling and what may be driving their perspective. When people feel that their emotions and concerns are validated, they're more likely to engage in constructive dialogue.

Find Common Ground
One of the most effective ways to resolve conflict is to identify areas of agreement or shared goals. Focusing on commonalities can help diffuse tension and shift the conversation toward finding solutions that benefit everyone.

Create a Win-Win Solution
Rather than framing conflict as a win-lose situation, strive for a solution where both parties feel satisfied with the outcome. Compromise may be necessary, but the goal should be to find a resolution that allows both sides to move forward positively.

THE IMPORTANCE OF ADDRESSING CONFLICT EARLY

One of the biggest mistakes leaders make is avoiding conflict. Hoping that issues will resolve themselves or waiting until things reach a boiling point can make conflicts more difficult to address. By tackling conflict early, you prevent small issues from turning into major problems and show your team that you are proactive and committed to maintaining a healthy working environment.

Prevents Escalation
Addressing conflict early on stops it from escalating into bigger issues. A minor disagreement can quickly spiral into resentment or damaged relationships if left unresolved. Nip problems in the bud before they grow.

Shows Commitment to Team Well-Being
When you take steps to resolve conflict promptly, you demonstrate to your team that their well-being and the team's harmony are priorities. This builds trust and shows that you care about maintaining a positive work environment.

NAVIGATING DIFFICULT CONVERSATIONS

Difficult conversations are an inevitable part of leadership. Whether you're addressing underperformance, providing feedback, or discussing sensitive topics, these conversations require both courage and tact. Here are strategies to navigate difficult conversations successfully:

Prepare in Advance
Before entering a difficult conversation, take the time to prepare. Consider what you need to say, the outcome you hope to achieve, and how the other person may react. Preparation helps you stay focused and composed during the conversation.

Be Direct but Compassionate
When delivering difficult feedback or addressing a sensitive issue, be clear and direct. Don't beat around the bush, but also be compassionate. It's possible to be honest without being harsh. Frame your feedback in a way that is constructive and focused on growth.

Use "I" Statements
When addressing conflict or giving feedback, use "I" statements to communicate your perspective without sounding accusatory. For example, instead of saying, "You never meet deadlines," say, "I've noticed that some deadlines have been missed, and I'd like to

understand how we can improve this moving forward."

Listen Actively

Difficult conversations should be a two-way street. Give the other person a chance to share their thoughts and feelings. Practise active listening by paying attention, nodding, and summarising what they've said to ensure you've understood their perspective.

Focus on Solutions

The goal of any difficult conversation is to find a way forward. Focus on identifying solutions rather than dwelling on the problem. For example, if you're addressing underperformance, discuss actionable steps for improvement rather than just highlighting what went wrong.

TURNING CONFLICT INTO AN OPPORTUNITY FOR GROWTH

Conflict can feel uncomfortable, but it's also an opportunity for growth—both for the individuals involved and for the team as a whole. When conflict is handled constructively, it can lead to:

Better Understanding: Conflict often stems from miscommunication or differences in perspective. Resolving conflict helps people understand each other better, leading to stronger relationships.

Improved Communication: Working through conflict encourages open, honest communication, which can improve team dynamics moving forward.

Innovation and Creativity: When different perspectives collide, it can spark new ideas and creative solutions. Conflict can be a driving force for innovation when handled productively.

Stronger Team Bonds: When conflicts are resolved, and difficult conversations are had, teams often come out stronger. Addressing issues head-on builds trust and respect within the team.

HOMEWORK: PRACTISING CONFLICT RESOLUTION AND DIFFICULT CONVERSATIONS

Conflict Reflection Exercise
Think about a recent conflict you've experienced in your professional life. Reflect on how the conflict arose and how it was resolved (or left unresolved). Write down what went well and what could have been handled differently. Identify one key takeaway from this reflection that you can apply to future conflicts.

Role-Playing Difficult Conversations
Partner with a colleague or friend to role-play a difficult conversation. Choose a real-life scenario, such as giving constructive feedback or addressing a disagreement. Practice delivering your message clearly and compassionately. Afterward, discuss what worked well and where you can improve.

Facilitating Conflict Resolution in a Team Setting
The next time a conflict arises within your team, take on the role of mediator. Use the steps outlined in this chapter to facilitate a resolution. Focus on creating an open dialogue, remaining

neutral, and finding a win-win solution.

CHAPTER 10: CONTINUOUS LEARNING AND SELF-IMPROVEMENT

Leadership is not a destination; it's a journey. The most successful leaders understand that they will never "arrive" at perfection but must continually evolve and adapt. In today's fast-paced, ever-changing world, the ability to learn, grow, and improve is more critical than ever before. What separates great leaders from average ones is their commitment to continuous learning and self-improvement.

The idea that "leaders are learners" isn't just a catchy phrase—it's a guiding principle for long-term success. Great leaders are those who recognize that, no matter how experienced they are, they can always become better. This chapter will explore why continuous learning is essential for leadership, how you can foster a mindset of growth, and specific strategies for investing in your own development as a leader.

WHY CONTINUOUS LEARNING IS ESSENTIAL FOR LEADERSHIP

Leadership is not a static skill set. It's a dynamic process that requires adapting to new challenges, technologies, and evolving team dynamics. The world is constantly changing, and the demands placed on leaders are growing more complex. Leaders who rely solely on their past knowledge and experience without seeking new learning opportunities risk becoming stagnant.

Here's why continuous learning is so important:

Staying Relevant in a Changing World
Industries evolve, and so do the skills required to lead within them. Leaders who don't make a conscious effort to stay updated with the latest trends, technologies, and best practices risk falling behind. For example, consider how rapidly technology has changed the way we work—leaders need to understand new tools, digital trends, and the implications of artificial intelligence (AI) to remain effective in the modern workplace.

Enhancing Problem-Solving Skills
The more you learn, the better equipped you are to tackle complex challenges. Leaders often face problems that don't have clear-cut solutions. Continuous learning helps you develop a broader

perspective and new approaches to problem-solving, enabling you to see issues from different angles and devise innovative solutions.

Building Emotional Intelligence

As we've explored earlier, emotional intelligence (EQ) is a cornerstone of effective leadership. Continuous self-improvement can help you further develop your EQ. Through learning and self-reflection, you gain deeper insights into your own behaviours, triggers, and reactions, which helps you manage your emotions better and lead with empathy.

Strengthening Leadership Capabilities

Leadership skills such as communication, conflict resolution, and decision-making can always be refined and improved. By investing in continuous learning, you can build upon these foundational skills, adapting them to different contexts and improving your overall effectiveness as a leader.

THE MINDSET OF CONTINUOUS LEARNING

For many, the greatest obstacle to continuous learning is their mindset. Some individuals believe that leadership is an inherent trait or something fixed, which leads them to avoid seeking new knowledge. However, effective leaders adopt a "growth mindset."

A growth mindset is the belief that your abilities and intelligence can be developed with effort, learning, and persistence. In contrast, a fixed mindset believes that your leadership skills are static and cannot be significantly improved. Leaders with a growth mindset are more open to feedback, willing to try new approaches, and see challenges as opportunities to grow.

EMBRACING HUMILITY AS A LEADER

Humility is a key aspect of a growth mindset. Being humble doesn't mean downplaying your strengths or shrinking in the face of challenges; rather, it means understanding that there is always room for improvement. Humble leaders don't see themselves as all-knowing but rather as lifelong learners who are open to new ideas and feedback.

Acknowledge What You Don't Know
A humble leader acknowledges their knowledge gaps and seeks out ways to fill them. If there's a particular area of leadership where you feel weak—whether it's managing remote teams, navigating diversity and inclusion, or developing technical acumen—recognize it, and seek resources or training to improve.

Be Open to Feedback
One of the best ways to continue learning is to solicit feedback from others. Ask for feedback from your peers, team members, or mentors. What do they see as your strengths? What areas could you improve on? Be open to hearing their perspectives and use their insights to guide your self-improvement efforts.

Surround Yourself with Smart People
Leaders should never feel threatened by working with people who know more than they do. In fact, surrounding yourself with individuals who have different expertise or perspectives can accelerate your learning. Being willing to ask questions, listen to others, and admit when you don't have all the answers fosters

both personal and professional growth.

STRATEGIES FOR CONTINUOUS LEARNING AND SELF-IMPROVEMENT

Now that we've covered the importance of continuous learning and adopting a growth mindset, let's explore practical strategies to incorporate learning and self-improvement into your leadership routine.

Set Clear Learning Goals
Just like setting performance goals for your team, setting learning goals for yourself ensures you stay on track. What areas of leadership do you want to improve? Do you want to enhance your public speaking skills, develop your ability to manage cross-functional teams, or better understand the financial aspects of your business? Identify these goals and make a plan to work on them.

Seek Out Mentors
Mentorship is one of the most effective ways to grow as a leader. Having someone more experienced to guide you, offer advice, and provide feedback can significantly accelerate your leadership development. Find mentors who can help you with specific areas of growth, whether it's within your organisation or an external network.

Engage in Continuous Learning Programs
There are many resources available to support continuous learning, from online courses to executive education programs. Platforms like Coursera, LinkedIn Learning, or industry-specific certifications can help you develop new skills or deepen your expertise in areas relevant to your leadership role.

Read Widely
One of the easiest ways to foster continuous learning is to read. Whether you're reading leadership books, industry publications, or thought pieces by respected leaders, keeping up with current ideas and perspectives will ensure you're always learning. Try to diversify your reading—don't just stick to topics you're already familiar with, but explore areas outside your expertise.

Attend Conferences and Workshops
Conferences, workshops, and seminars are excellent opportunities to gain new insights, network with other leaders, and hear from industry experts. Attending these events also exposes you to new trends and best practices in leadership, ensuring you stay up-to-date in your field.

Reflect Regularly
Learning from experience is one of the most powerful forms of growth. Set aside time for regular reflection on your leadership performance. After completing a project, handling a difficult conversation, or navigating a conflict, reflect on what went well and what didn't. What lessons can you draw from these experiences? How will you handle similar situations in the future? This kind of introspection promotes self-awareness and allows you to continuously improve your leadership approach.

OVERCOMING CHALLENGES IN CONTINUOUS LEARNING

The path to continuous learning isn't always smooth. It's common to face challenges along the way, whether it's time constraints, feeling overwhelmed, or struggling to find motivation. Here's how to overcome these obstacles:

Prioritise Learning
As a busy leader, time is often your biggest challenge. However, continuous learning needs to be a priority. Block out time in your schedule specifically for learning activities—whether that's reading, taking a course, or reflecting on your leadership performance.

Stay Curious
Approach each day with curiosity. When faced with a challenge, ask yourself, "What can I learn from this?" Rather than focusing solely on outcomes, view challenges as learning opportunities that contribute to your growth as a leader.

Don't Fear Failure
Part of continuous learning involves making mistakes and learning from them. Don't let the fear of failure stop you from trying new things. Embrace failure as a valuable part of the

learning process and use it to fuel your improvement.

THE RIPPLE EFFECT OF CONTINUOUS LEARNING ON YOUR TEAM

One of the greatest benefits of your commitment to continuous learning is the example you set for your team. When your team sees that you are constantly striving to improve, they are more likely to adopt a similar mindset. By modelling a commitment to growth, you create a culture of learning within your organisation.

Inspire a Learning Culture
Encourage your team to seek out learning opportunities for themselves. This could include offering professional development programs, supporting attendance at industry conferences, or creating space for peer learning and knowledge sharing. A team that is committed to learning will be more adaptable, innovative, and motivated.

Provide Learning Opportunities
Great leaders don't just focus on their own learning but are also committed to the development of their team members. Create opportunities for your team to grow by offering them challenging assignments, mentorship, or access to learning resources.

HOMEWORK: DEVELOPING A CONTINUOUS LEARNING PLAN

Self-Assessment of Learning Needs
Reflect on your current leadership skills and identify areas where you could benefit from further development. Write down at least three specific leadership areas you want to improve in the next year. These could be skills like decision-making, emotional intelligence, or communication.

Create a Learning Plan
Based on your self-assessment, create a learning plan for the next six months. What specific actions will you take to develop these skills? This might include reading books, enrolling in a course, attending a workshop, or finding a mentor. Make your plan actionable, with clear timelines and goals.

Seek Feedback
Ask at least one colleague or team member for feedback on your leadership performance. Use their insights to refine your learning plan and identify any blind spots you might not have been aware of.

CONCLUSION: BECOMING A PRO-LEVEL LEADER

Becoming a pro-level leader is not about having all the answers or being the most skilled person in the room. It's about understanding that leadership is a craft, one that requires dedication, practice, and continuous learning. Leadership is both an art and a science, involving not only strategy and decision-making but also emotional intelligence, empathy, and human connection.

Throughout this book, we've explored many facets of leadership, from understanding your personal leadership style to mastering communication, building trust, and motivating your team. We've discussed how great leaders don't shy away from conflict, how they delegate effectively, and how they inspire others to reach their full potential. We've also examined the importance of continuous learning—leaders who are constantly growing are the ones who can adapt, innovate, and thrive in any situation.

But what does it really mean to "lead like a pro"? The truth is, professional-level leadership isn't about a title, years of experience, or how many people report to you. It's about the mindset and behaviours you cultivate, the way you show up every day, and your commitment to making a positive impact on those around you. Pro-level leaders are not only focused on achieving their goals; they are also deeply committed to helping others succeed.

THE JOURNEY OF LEADERSHIP

If there's one thing to take away from this book, it's that leadership is a journey, not a destination. No one becomes a perfect leader overnight. It's an ongoing process of self-reflection, learning, adapting, and evolving. Every experience—whether it's a success or a failure—is an opportunity to grow and become a better leader.

Great leaders are curious. They ask questions, seek new perspectives, and aren't afraid to challenge their own assumptions. They know that growth comes from stepping out of their comfort zone and embracing change. Even the most seasoned leaders understand that they will never stop learning because the world around them is always evolving.

The journey to becoming a pro-level leader is filled with challenges. There will be moments when you question your decisions, when you feel uncertain, or when you encounter setbacks. These are not signs of weakness but opportunities to strengthen your leadership muscles. How you respond to these moments will define your growth. Instead of avoiding difficult situations, embrace them. Each challenge you face will build your resilience, sharpen your problem-solving skills, and deepen your understanding of leadership.

THE CORE TRAITS OF PRO-LEVEL LEADERSHIP

As we've explored throughout this book, there are certain core traits that define pro-level leadership. While every leader is unique and brings their own style and strengths to the table, these fundamental qualities are what separate good leaders from great ones.

Self-Awareness
Pro-level leaders have a deep understanding of themselves. They are aware of their strengths and weaknesses, and they know how their actions and behaviours impact others. This self-awareness allows them to be intentional about their leadership and adapt their approach based on the needs of their team and the situation at hand.

Emotional Intelligence (EQ)
EQ is the foundation of great leadership. Leaders who are emotionally intelligent can connect with others on a human level, understand their emotions, and respond with empathy and care. They build trust and loyalty because their teams feel valued and understood. They are also better equipped to navigate conflict, manage stress, and lead through uncertainty.

Communication Skills
Communication is the lifeblood of leadership. Pro-level leaders

excel at both listening and speaking. They know how to articulate their vision, provide clear direction, and give constructive feedback. They also listen actively to their team members, ensuring that everyone's voice is heard and that they feel a sense of belonging and purpose within the organisation.

Integrity and Trustworthiness
Great leaders lead by example. They are honest, transparent, and consistent in their actions. Trust is the bedrock of leadership, and pro-level leaders understand that building trust requires time, effort, and authenticity. They follow through on their commitments and are always guided by a strong sense of ethics and values.

Vision and Strategic Thinking
Pro-level leaders have a clear vision for the future, but they don't stop at having big ideas. They know how to translate that vision into actionable steps and inspire their teams to execute on it. Strategic thinking allows them to anticipate challenges, seize opportunities, and make informed decisions that drive long-term success.

THE ROLE OF SELF-IMPROVEMENT

No matter where you are on your leadership journey, there's always room for improvement. The best leaders are those who are constantly seeking to grow, evolve, and become better versions of themselves. Continuous learning and self-improvement are non-negotiable for pro-level leaders.

Self-improvement begins with self-reflection. Take time to regularly assess your leadership performance. What are you doing well? What areas need improvement? Be honest with yourself and seek feedback from others. Remember, self-improvement is not about being perfect—it's about striving for progress and making consistent efforts to grow.

Great leaders are also lifelong learners. They read, attend workshops, seek mentors, and invest in their personal and professional development. They understand that in order to lead others effectively, they must first lead themselves.

EMPOWERING OTHERS

One of the hallmarks of a pro-level leader is their ability to empower others. Leadership is not about being in control or having all the power—it's about lifting others up and helping them reach their potential. Pro-level leaders create environments where people feel safe to take risks, share their ideas, and grow.

Empowering others means delegating effectively, trusting your team to take ownership of their work, and providing them with the resources and support they need to succeed. It also means being a mentor and coach, guiding others on their own leadership journey. When you invest in the growth of those around you, you not only create stronger teams but also contribute to a culture of leadership within your organisation.

LEAVING A LEGACY

At the end of the day, leadership is about leaving a positive legacy. When people reflect on their experiences working with you, what will they remember? Pro-level leaders leave a lasting impact not because of the positions they held or the projects they completed but because of how they made people feel, how they inspired others to grow, and the culture they fostered within their teams.

Legacy is built over time through consistent actions. It's about leading with integrity, building strong relationships, and making decisions that prioritise the well-being of others. Great leaders don't just focus on the present—they think about the future. They understand that their leadership has a ripple effect, influencing the careers and lives of those they lead, and they take that responsibility seriously.

YOUR LEADERSHIP JOURNEY

Becoming a pro-level leader is within your reach. It's not reserved for a select few—it's a path that anyone willing to put in the effort can walk. It requires dedication, self-awareness, and a commitment to continuous learning and growth.

As you move forward, remember that leadership is a privilege. It's an opportunity to make a meaningful impact on the lives of others, to inspire, guide, and empower. Every day presents new opportunities to practise the skills you've learned and to refine your leadership approach.

Whether you're leading a team of two or two hundred, your role as a leader matters. You have the power to create positive change, to drive results, and to build a culture where people feel valued and motivated. Stay curious, stay humble, and never stop growing.

YOUR LEADERSHIP HOMEWORK: REFLECT AND PLAN FOR GROWTH

Reflect on Your Leadership Journey
Take some time to reflect on your growth as a leader so far. What have been your biggest successes? What challenges have you faced? How have these experiences shaped you as a leader? Write down your reflections and consider how you can continue to grow.

Create a Leadership Development Plan
Based on what you've learned from this book, create a leadership development plan for the next six months. Identify specific areas you want to improve and set actionable goals. For example, if you want to work on your communication skills, you might set a goal to attend a communication workshop or seek feedback from your team.

Seek Out a Mentor or Coach
Consider finding a mentor or coach who can help you on your leadership journey. Having someone to guide and support you can accelerate your growth and provide valuable insights.

In closing, becoming a pro-level leader is not about perfection. It's about progress, growth, and making a positive impact on the people and organisations you lead. By committing to continuous learning, leading with integrity, and empowering others, you can elevate your leadership and truly lead like a pro. The journey is ongoing, but with dedication and purpose, you will continue to grow into the leader you aspire to be.

www.ingramcontent.com/pod-product-compliance
Lightning Source LLC
Chambersburg PA
CBHW050304230526
45471CB00005B/2005